The Day of Judgement

Our Unalienable Responsibility

The Day of Judgement

Our Unalienable Responsibility

by SYED MUKARRAM

ISBN: 978-0578-77222-6

Contents

Dedicated to Prophet Adam, the last person born before the trumpet is blown to end this world, and everybody in between

Preface

For at least twenty-five years, I was trying to write a book on this topic but never could gather the courage to actually write it—the reason being firstly that I am an engineer by profession, not a writer, and secondly because the topic seems to be very religious, and writing a book on religion is like touching the wounds of an injured person. I was always told never to talk politics or religion, especially at your school or at your job. With this mindset, it is obvious why it took me twenty-five years to write this book.

Not a day goes by in my life when I don't think about the Day of Judgement. Sometimes in the midst of a party, I pause for a second and start to imagine that if the Day of Judgement were to happen right now, everybody would lose all that they think so important in their lives and would be gathering to give an account of how they used their power, their money, and their time. All of a sudden, people will no longer be laughing at jokes but will be busy finding out who did wrong to them, and how they could get an advantage of some tiny little thing over somebody so that they could snatch a good deed from them or transfer a bad deed to them.

When the coronavirus pandemic hit, the whole world went through the kind of sudden change I used to imagine might happen. All of a sudden, the country that used to run at sixty-five miles per hour was at a zero-miles-per-hour speed. The never-sleeping airports were silent and empty. All the fast-moving lives were at standstills. The other very unusual thing that happened was what used to be a regular excuse of "not having time to do this or to do that" was no longer an excuse. We were inside our homes with almost all the avenues of our leisure shut down. If I use the phrase "This came as a blessing," many will be upset—and they should be, due to the fact that many lost their lives—but it certainly came as an opportunity to evaluate ourselves. The sudden change in the lifestyle of every single person was an opportunity to pause and think that the lifestyle we were so used to was merely a dummy lifestyle. This also gave me an opportunity to gather courage and start writing this book.

I did not write this book to be an industry standard. There is no scholarly research behind this book. This book is not about which religion is saying what about the Day of Judgement. This book is about the Day of Judgement that is certain to happen. The emphasis is on its happening and requesting the readers to prepare for it. The method I adopted in this book is to understand the Day of Judgement using common sense as much as possible. Of course, the root of the Day of Judgement lies in religion. When it comes to religion, there will be many differences of opinion, and I wanted to avoid going into those differences.

This book is not meant to be a prophecy or an exact play-by-play description of the events of Judgement Day. The Day of Judgement may occur the way it is described in these pages, or it might not. No person can know for sure. However, one thing is sure: Judgement Day will occur. The purpose of this book is merely to spark a discussion around how we choose to conduct ourselves today in order to face our spiritual futures without fear or regret. While Judgement

Day is often portrayed solely as an occasion to be feared or dreaded, I hope it will also bring you some comfort. If you have ever been cheated, defeated, or wronged by someone, you can find peace knowing that those people will be punished for their actions—even if they are never held accountable or brought to justice while they are alive.

I hope to offer you practical ways to prepare for the Day of Judgement in your day-to-day lives through a mixture of principles and examples you can apply to your circumstances.

This book is for you if you are Jewish. This book is for you if you are Christian. This book is for you if you are Hindu, Muslim, Mormon, atheist, or if you practice (or do *not* practice) any other faith.

I have to admit that in spite of trying hard not to be influenced by my beliefs, I could not keep this book as unbiased as I wanted it to be. I am a Muslim, and the Day of Judgement is the most important cornerstone of Islam. I wanted to show the importance of this event to everybody if I could without preaching Islam to them. I understand we are leaving in very tough times as far as religion is concerned. The attack of 9/11, the Middle East conflict, and so many other recent religious conflicts going on all over the world means this may not be a good time to share something that may be important for everybody. As I mentioned earlier, these were the same fears that were stopping me from writing this book. After overcoming those fears, I still have to deal with a story that is so embedded in Islam, and to take it out and show it to everybody is not an easy task. Therefore the readers will see places where I used Islamic concepts as tools to show them how things will be during the Day of Judgement. I tried to keep them as much as possible inside the territory of common sense. I hope the readers will understand my difficulty and will ignore any such biases and still focus on the core of this book: why the Day of Judgement is necessary and why it will happen.

It is also very important for me to include a disclaimer here. As I mentioned earlier, this book is to open a discussion about the Day of Judgement, not to close a case on the Day of Judgement. None of the readers can bring this book on the Day of Judgement and try to claim that this book misguided them in their preparation for this day or misguided them in any other possible way. The reader has a responsibility to go deep into this topic and find out the basic criteria that will be applied on the Day of Judgement with respect to their religion. It is the responsibility of the reader to find a pathway to the final success on the Day of Judgement through their own beliefs. It is not possible for me do evaluate the compatibility of the Day of Judgement with the beliefs of every single reader of this book.

The intention of this book is to firstly convince the reader that the Day of Judgement will happen and secondly to provide the readers as many tools as possible to prepare for this day. Many religions may say that there is no success on the Day of Judgement without actually following the concepts of their religion. Here, I totally avoided going into such claims. Let me give you an analogy of what I am trying to do here. If all the different car companies are claiming that the journey to certain place is very tough and only their car can safely take you through the journey, and that you can successfully reach your destination by only using their car, what I am trying to do is, for whatever car company you choose, to make sure you have certain tools and enough food if something happens to the car on its way to the destination. These tools will help you keep fixing the car during the journey. I hope and pray that you will still be able to reach your destination safely with the help of these tools and that during the delays, you still have some food to eat and survive. After reaching the destination, you can react to whether your decision of using a certain car was good or not. Or you may forget everything once you are home safely. The best possible car may have all these tools built in; however, having some extra tools may not be a bad idea just to be over-prepared for this tough journey.

I understand this topic itself is very difficult to universalize. I may not be the right person to write this book. But it is worth trying. Let's turn the page, and let's start the discussion.

Introduction

This book is for you if you want to find out whether there will be such a thing known as the Day of Judgement. This book is for you if you want to know why there is a need for this event, and why this world becomes totally absurd without this event. These were the questions I was asking myself, and during my entire life, I have been able to gather some of the answers to these questions.

As a Muslim from India, I was lucky to see many religions in action. I can even say that to an Indian Muslim, understanding all the major religions is much easier. Islam is an Abrahamic religion, along with Judaism and Christianity. Adherents to these religions comprise almost half the world's population. The Quran talks so much about all the prophets of Judaism and Christianity that every Muslim is aware of all of them. In fact Muslims consider all the prophets of Judaism and Christianity as prophets of Islam, just as Christians consider the Jewish prophets their prophets. Muslims also believe in Jesus Christ as the Messiah. If Muslims are asked, "Who is the most righteous woman of all time?" they will reply, "Mary, the mother of Jesus Christ." There is a chapter in the Quran named after Mary.

India is also the birthplace of many religions. Hinduism and Buddhism originated here. Adherents to these religions comprise almost a quarter of the world's population. I grew up in the midst of these Abrahamic and Indian religions. I was also very lucky to be raised in a very religious family, a mixed Sunni and Shia family. Relatives further gave me an advantage to understand the religions. I attended school run by the Methodist Church. Every day the school used to start with prayer service, and every student had to attend the service. The majority of the students were Hindu, and a substantial minority was Muslim. Neither of them had any problem attending a Christian prayer service. My personal home tutor was a Brahmin (the uppermost class of Hindus in charge of religious matters), and half my time with him was spent in discussing Hindu stories and concepts of Hinduism. I am a lifelong student. After coming to the United States of America, I attended several universities, including the University of Maryland at College Park and the University of Maryland at Baltimore County. Many of my teachers were Catholic and Jewish. I have learned so much from teachers who belonged to so many different religions. The reason for mentioning these facts is to tell my readers that it was very natural for me to write a book I think will help readers of any religion.

I have divided the book into two parts. In the first part, I want to establish the basics of the Day of Judgement. In the second part, I wish to provide tools to prepare for this huge event.

I started the first part with a chapter on God. If at all there is going to be a Day of Judgement, it has to be under an all-powerful God. I wanted to discuss that this massive event is only possible under a very powerful God who is the God of every single creature that exists in this universe. In the second chapter, I wanted to establish the human being as a creature who is accountable for every act this creature performs. Major religions, especially Judaism and Islam, say that there are two different accountabilities—one is toward God, and next is toward fellow human beings. In Judaism sins between people are considered more severe than the sins between individuals and God. Yom Kippur, the main day of repentance in Judaism, can be used for repenting of all the sins between individuals and God but cannot be used as repentance between individuals and other fellow humans. That can be achieved only by appeasing the person who was offended. According to Islam, God can forgive anything but will not forgive a person who adds any other god or gods with Him (the only one God). In other words, oneness of God is a basic tenant of Islam. However, when it comes to the dealings of one person with fellow human beings, God will not interfere between them. What does this mean? This means that if one human being has done anything—good or bad—to another human being, then there is nothing God can do to satisfy the matter except to have a Day of Judgement and give everybody an equal opportunity to settle the matter. The best thing God can also do, I think, is that if he loves one of the persons involved in the dispute, he could offer a great reward to the other person if that person can let the person whom God loves go unpunished. However, it will be only in the hands of the person who got hurt by the person whom God loves to accept or deny the offer.

In the third chapter, I explore what kind of event the Day of Judgement is going to be. Finally, in the fourth chapter, I close the first part with a discussion of why the Day of Judgement is necessary. Using common sense, I showed that this event is necessary, and if there is not going to be a Day of Judgement, then everything in this world becomes meaningless.

In the second part, I explore the tools that we can use to prepare for the Day of Judgement. The most important of them is to understand our foremost unalienable responsibility: that is to prepare for the Day of Judgement. The first chapter in the second part is dedicated to understanding this unalienable responsibility. The second chapter is dedicated to understanding our past in order to bring our current standing on the right footing. Similarly, the third chapter explores how we can act in the present to secure success on the Day of Judgement. Finally, in the fourth chapter of part two, I explore the future. Prepare for the future in order to have a successful Day of Judgement.

The overall intention of this book is to inform readers that the Day of Judgement is coming. Everything will boil down to this day, when every human being will have to answer for all of his or her deeds. Whatever you did, good or bad, will come out, and you will be rewarded for the good and punished for the bad. This Judgement will take place in the presence of all humanity. Every single human being born here in this world will be there.

Let me close this introduction so that the readers may start the journey to understanding this most important day, the Day of Judgement.

Part One

Basics of the Day of Judgement

The first and foremost requirement of the Day of Judgement is that there must be a God. What will actually happen on the Day of Judgement is that God will take control of everything that existed in this universe. It is true that God already has control over everything right now; however, there are some intermediary people with money and power. Now God has declared that all these activities should stop, and everybody should gather to find out what they were doing. The reason is that humans were created as responsible creatures. With responsibility comes accountability.

During humans' stay in this world, whatever good deeds they were doing were going into a positive account, and whatever bad deeds they were doing were going into a negative account. On the Day of Judgement, all humans will find out their balances. Many humans were secretly deceiving other humans. All secrets will be brought out so that they will be judged. That day will be full of surprises. Every single human being who spent a life in this world will be there. If you have a positive account, that day will be full of joy. Anybody could meet with all their ancestors, from their father to their grandfather, up to Adam. You will be able to play videos of your life and recall all these days you spent in this world. I hope everybody will increase their positive deeds so that the day will be a joyous day.

This day is inevitable, and without it, everything would become senseless. In the following four chapters, we will explore whether there is a God, what the accountability of humans is, what will be the Day of Judgement be like, and why is it necessary.

Chapter 1

Is There a God?

More than half the population believes there is a God. Incredibly, there are many examples of the same stories of God's work being known across the world, even by cultures that have never interacted with the others. Take the story of Moses parting the Red Sea. Moses was able to take the Jews out of Egypt without any violence because of God's power. The Red Sea was parted, making a way for the people to leave Egypt. We can know the story is true because the same story is told in the Quran two thousand years after it happened, in the same way it was told in the Bible and in the Torah. Even though no one in the Mecca area had heard of Moses, the Prophet Muhammad was given the same story. The story about Moses's departure from Egypt was revealed by God alone. Isn't this proof that there is a God?

Regarding the question of whether we can see God, the answer is that no one can see God. The only human who came close was Moses. When he asked to see God, God told him to come up on a mountain. When God let His holiness come upon the mountain, the mountain crumbled, and Moses fell unconscious. Our bodies simply are not capable of seeing God. As Aisha, the wife of the Prophet Muhammad, said, "If someone is telling you they saw God, that person is lying." Adam might have seen God when he was in paradise. After coming down to the earth, I am pretty sure even Adam never saw God.

If we cannot see God, how can we know God exists? There are simply some things in life about which we cannot say, "I won't believe it until I see it." How can anyone show the feeling of happiness or joy or pain to another person? These things cannot be seen. When someone says he is in pain, you cannot see the pain. As with the existence of God, there is only belief. If you reflect on the story of your own life, you'll see places where things were not possible, but they happened anyway, and you'll know the cause was the hand of God at work. Almost everyone has a story where they say, "There was no power other than God that did that for me."

No one can see God. You can only have the stories of His work in the past, the feelings of His presence, and the knowledge of your life and circumstances. If you take an honest look, there will be something from your past that will show you God exists and is working in your life.

Not only is there God, but He is also in charge of every single major, minor, and micro creature that exists in this universe. The Day of Judgement is the most magnificent and biggest incident that can happen to this universe. Not only will all the human beings who ever lived in this world be there, but every single creature that ever existed in this universe will also be there. In order for the God to bring the Day of Judgement upon us, He will have to fulfill certain conditions.

Firstly, the God of one person will have to be God of every person. I think He is. If the God of one person is different from the God of another person, then the other person will have to be different, like cars from different companies are different. I understand not every human being is similar to every other human being. That is not the question. The question is whether one person from one race can marry a person from other race; the answer is yes, because they belong to the same God. Irrespective of race and gender, we are all created equal. All humans, regardless of where they are in the world, are built the same way: we have hearts and we have brains, medicine affects us the same way, and so on. If all human beings are similar in all important aspects, then the God of all of them should be the same.

Secondly, the God of human beings should also be the God of every other creature that exists in this universe. If the Day of Judgement has to happen, there must be a God who can make it happen. This God will have to be the God of not only one human being but the God of all human beings. Not only that, but this God will also have to be the God of every single creature that exists in this universe. This is the reason that humans will have to answer about all resources they used in this world. What does this mean? This means that human beings rely on many sources that are not just human beings; for example, human beings eat wheat, rice, and many other things. If the God of wheat or rice is different than the God of human beings, then it will be a problem. If the God of human beings is not in agreement with the God of wheat or rice, then the wheat or rice will not be allowed to be consumed by humans by the God of wheat or rice. It is not happening this way anywhere. All nature is working hand in hand with all its components. Therefore, the God of human beings is the God of all creatures that exist in this universe.

Let us again go back to the story of Moses. At his birth, his mom put him in a basket and let him go into the river. God guided the river to take Moses to Pharaoh's palace. God could guide the river because the river belongs to Him. Later, when Moses was crossing the Sahara Desert, the most dangerous desert of the world, he was able to because God made that desert at peace for him. God was able to do this because that desert belongs to Him. Finally, Moses and his people were allowed to cross the Red Sea when God parted the Red Sea. God could do this because God is the owner of all the seas. Now let us go to the story of Abraham, when he was thrown into the fire. The fire was made at peace for Abraham by God. God could do this because the God of Abraham is also the God of fire. Or we can go to the story of Jonah, when he was swallowed by a fish, and it delivered him safely to the shore. God was able to do this because He is not only the God of Jonah but also the God of fishes. If we go to any major university, we will see the departments of various studies and humans learning about all the different fields. This is because God is running every single field based on laws that can be understood by humans.

Because humans belong to same God as do these different fields, humans can learn about them. There is not a single field where one can say, "You cannot learn this field because the God of this field is different than the God of you humans." Therefore, it is quite clear that the God of humans is the God of every single creature that exists. The God of humans is the God of everything. When I say "everything," I mean everything that we can see and that is beyond the reach of our vision. In order for the Day of Judgement to happen, God should be the God of every single creature that exists in this universe, including human beings and nonhuman beings. The God should be the God of all the generations, from Adam to the last person who will live in this world. The God should be the God of everything that we see and everything that is beyond the reach of our vision. If there is such a God, then only the Day of Judgement is possible. And if there is such a God, then there will be the Day of Judgement.

Takeaways

1. There is a God.
2. It is not possible for humans to see God.
3. Everyone's life is full of stories showing the work of God.
4. Nature is working in harmony because God is God of everything that exists.
5. If there is a God, then there is the Day of Judgement.

Chapter 2

Humans Are Accountable

Human beings are the only creatures who have the ability to comprehend. As the poet Rumi said, "You are not a drop in the ocean. You are the entire ocean in a drop." The best possible creations are human beings. We don't even realize the extent of our abilities. Despite all the incredible advances in science that have been made, we still don't fully understand how the human brain works, let alone the entire human body.

There is a great saying: "With great power comes great responsibility." Human beings have been put in charge of the universe. That is why we were given the mental capacity to understand $E=mc^2$, physics, astronomy, all the branches of science, and our place in existence. We were given a position of leadership among all the creatures of the earth. It is our duty to understand Judgement Day because everything in human history will come down to that day.

Why we were given the ability to comprehend? This is for a reason. That reason is to understand that there will be consequences for our actions. Accountability should be the easiest thing to understand for a human being, as it is seen throughout the life of anyone. Right from kindergarten through high school to college to a professional career, accountability can be found everywhere. Humans are continuously monitored by their fellow human beings just to make them accountable. So how can we then expect that there will not be a final accountability on the Day of Judgement? One can wonder why there is any need for the final accountability when all of us have gone through so many accountabilities throughout our lives. Well, the answer may be that all the previous accountabilities were not error proof. There might even be bias with those accountabilities. Those accountabilities were random. The criteria were different from place to place. Finally, those accountabilities were human. The final accountability will be by God Himself. It will be flawless. It will be universal. Finally, it will be for the whole life of every human being. Every single second they lived in this world is prone to accountability. Human beings will have to answer about their good or bad deeds. They will have to answer how they utilized the resources they were provided by God. They will have to answer how they acquired their resources. Did they use legitimate methods or illegitimate methods? How did they treat other creatures that were at their disposal?

The major components to which humans are accountable may be many. The most important of them are relationships, time, money, knowledge, and power. These five accountabilities pretty much sum up 90 percent of the total accountabilities. Of course there will be many minor responsibilities for which we are all accountable on a daily basis, such as cleanliness with respect to our bodies, our clothes, our homes, our lawns, or any other thing we own. Because everything affects every other thing, that is why it is important to handle every responsibility promptly. Let us explore the abovementioned five areas to which every human will be held accountable.

1. *Relationships:*

   What did you do with the relationships you were trusted with? This question will be very important on the Day of Judgement. The first and foremost relationship is our relationship with our Creator. As mentioned earlier, Abrahamic religions put lots of emphasis on our relationship with God. The first and the second commandments of the Ten Commandments deal with our relationship with God. The next very important relationship to which we are accountable is our relationship with our own bodies. How did we treat our body? Did we give it the respect it deserves? Did we keep it healthy and clean? Therefore we have to be mindful of how we treat ourselves. The relationship with our parents is another important relationship. Did you take care of your parents when they needed you? The other important relationships that we have to take care of are our relationships with our spouses, with our children, with our neighbors, with our government, and with our environment.

These questions will be asked: Did you give all the attention to your spouse and to your children they needed? Did you treat your neighbors well? Did you obey the rules of the road? Did you take your civic duty seriously?

2. *Time:*

When it comes to time, these are the questions that might be asked: What did you do with your time? Where did you spend time? How much time did you spend in prayer? How much time did you spend seeking knowledge? Did you give enough time to your parents and family? How much time did you spend watching television? Why did you spend so much time watching professional sports?

3. *Money:*

"Trace the money trail" will be the slogan of the Day of Judgement. How did you earn your money? Were the methods legitimate? How did you spend your money? Did you spend money on your parents? Did you spend money on the education of yourself and your children? Did you spend money on the poor and on the needy?

4. *Knowledge:*

These are the questions relevant to knowledge: How did you utilize the knowledge given to you? Did you use your knowledge to provide solutions to problems? Did you use your knowledge to help others gain knowledge? Did you spread the knowledge that you had?

5. *Power:*

With power comes accountability. These are the questions relevant to power: What did you do with the power that was bestowed upon you? Did you help the weak to get their rights? Did you treat the poor as equal to the rich or give preference to the rich over the poor? How did you treat the animals over whom you had power?

We were not placed here to fool everyone, to live a deceiving life and then escape. We cannot make decisions randomly on selfish whims or desires alone. Everything we do is being recorded, even the decisions we make when we think we're alone. God will hold us accountable for our actions toward others, the good as well as the bad. God will not say, "This person has the right to harm another" because the person comes from a particular geographic area, is descended from a certain family, has a certain job title, or has a larger amount of money, or for any other reason.

Even if we are not punished during our lifetimes for misdeeds, we will face the consequences after death when we are judged. Everything will be brought out into the open.

All the religions differentiate sins into two classes: major sins and minor sins. Hinduism and Buddhism start without recognizing any. But when we search deeply, there are sins such as killing a Brahmin (uppermost class of Hindus in charge of religious matters) in Hinduism, or killing an Arhat (a person who has achieved Nirvana) in Buddhism, considered to be major sins. Accountability will be much greater when it comes to the major sins. The Ten Commandments are the most important commandments with respect to major sins. All the religions either directly or indirectly and either completely or partially agree on these Ten Commandments. I think this is the most basic document to which humans are accountable.

The other important reason why humans are accountable is that humans are trusted with the power to choose between many options. Their accountability becomes a necessity after this entrustment. Humans can choose to ignore their responsibilities. However, they will be held accountable for ignoring their responsibilities. Humans can choose to go down the hill because it is easier to go down the hill, as gravity is working in favor of going down the hill. But the goalpost is set on top of the hill. Going down the hill is not going to help achieve the goal. Going up the hill requires effort, as gravity is working against going up the hill. The result of this effort is achieving the goal. Still, somebody can choose to go down the hill, but they will be held accountable for going down the hill when the goalpost was on top of the hill. Of course this is just an analogy. It would be great if the goalpost were also set at the bottom of the hill; then we could achieve the goal without huge effort. However, most of life's goals are set on top of the hill.

Takeaways

1. Humans are the only creatures who can comprehend.
2. This ability is to understand that they are accountable.
3. The other important reason humans are accountable is they have ability to choose.
4. Humans are responsible for each and every action they do in this world.
5. On the Day of Judgement, humans will be asked what they did with their relationships, time, money, knowledge, and power.
6. Depending on major or minor sins, the accountability varies.

Chapter 3

What Is Judgement Day—
and Why Should I Care?

If you take nothing else from this book, I want you to walk away with the knowledge that Judgement Day is coming. It will be as real as this book in your hands, as real as the ground under your feet, and as real as everything you see, feel, and touch right now. One day you'll be standing and thinking, "Everything in my life was leading up to this—why didn't I do more?" People will say, "Oh, people used to talk about this, but we didn't really do anything about it." One day there will be nothing but accounting for your actions. You never know when it will happen.

The most absurd thing that could ever happen would be this world without the Day of Judgement. Everything in this world would be a joke if there were no Day of Judgement. The good or bad wouldn't mean anything if there were no Day of Judgement. It would be OK to fool anyone as long as they didn't know that you were fooling them. No need to take care of your parents. It would be OK to steal as long as nobody saw you. But it is not like this, my dear friend. There is all-watching and ever-watching God, and He will bring us to the Day of Judgement. I can't emphasize this enough: Judgement Day is coming, and we must prepare.

What Will Judgement Day Be Like?

There are many differing interpretations of Judgement Day. Will the world erupt in flames? Will everyone ascend or descend to be judged? Will your heart be weighed on a scale against a feather? Will each person go one at a time, like a never-ending line at the airport, or will it all happen to everyone simultaneously? If we explore different religions, every one of them will have a particular version of the Day of Judgement. If you want to know in detail what Judaism, Christianity, Islam, Hinduism, Buddhism, and any other religion say about the Day of Judgement, religious books like the Torah, the Bible, the Quran, the Vedas, and the Tripitaka will definitely help you understand this day. The internet is also full of articles that can help you find that out. The bottom line is that every major religion believes in a Day of Judgement in some form or other. All the Abrahamic religions (Judaism, Christianity, and Islam) have a strong concept of life after death. Of course they are not united in one similar form, but they know that there is a Judgement Day coming. The similarities and the differences of these Abrahamic religions are out of the scope of this book. Some other religions like Hinduism and Buddhism believe in reincarnation. One thing is sure: every human being dies—for that matter, every living organism dies. It is my understanding that when the scholars of Hinduism and Buddhism saw that the general population is not in a position to understand the concept of life after death, they started saying that after you die, you take a form in your next life. They somehow wanted the population to at least understand that there are consequences to good as well as bad. Therefore they started preaching that if you do good, then in your next life, you will be able to live peacefully or take a form of a human being. Otherwise, if you do bad deeds, then in your next life, you will take the form of some inferior animal or some other inferior creature. Both Hinduism and Buddhism believe in *swarg* (heaven) and *Narg* (hell), which are similar to Abrahamic religions. Again, the actual discussion on reincarnation is out of the scope of this book. Everything is possible with God. He can use reincarnation if He wants. There might be cases of reincarnation happening in this world.

One thing we must understand that whatever way the Day of Judgement will fall upon us, it will fall on all humanity in a similar way. It cannot be different for one religion and different for another. If every human being is living in this world as part of one humanity, then how can there be different procedures for different humans depending on their religion? If a Muslim did something wrong to a Hindu, then who will decide whether that Muslim should be punished according to Hindu belief and should be reincarnated or should be punished according to Muslim belief and should be judged on the Day of Judgement? And if reincarnation is the procedure, then it should be for all humanity, not just for Hindus or just for Buddhists.

For any disputes here in this world, both parties have to be there. Similarly, both parties have to be present during the Day of Judgement if there is a dispute that has to be solved. The results may vary; one person can forgive another person, or one person may have to give one good deed to the affected person or take a bad deed from the affected person. But more than anything, the process itself will be enough for the affected person to see that the other person was held accountable. And imagine if somebody has committed some kind of injustice to you, and when that person dies, he or she was judged without you knowing anything. Even if that person had to pay a penalty of doing injustice to you, it will be useless until you know that that person was punished for doing injustice to you. Even if you were informed of the punishment, that will not be gratifying to you because you were not a part of the process that penalized the other person. That is why both parties have to be present—especially when a person who was weak, poor, and powerless in this world will stand next to a person who was strong, powerful, and rich in this world, and demand that they be given a chance to treat the second person the same way that person treated them in this world or insult the person the same way the second person used to insult the first person in this world. The most important thing is that it is not about anybody who committed injustice; it is about the other person upon whom the injustice has been done. And only the Day of Judgement can fulfill such a demand, bringing both of them on the same platform. The purpose of this book is to make readers aware that there is definitely going to be such a Day of Judgement.

To make sure we're on the same page for the sake of this discussion, this is what Judgement Day will entail:

Everyone came into this world through their mother's womb. It took nine months for them to be delivered in this state. When they leave this world, they also go back to a place. In Islam, that place is known as Barzakh: a place people wait between death and Judgement Day. For the people there, Judgement Day seems to happen in an instant. It's like going to sleep—when they wake up for Judgement Day, they will feel as if no time has passed. Even if thousands or millions of years pass after you die, Judgement Day will seem to come upon you quickly, in the blink of an eye.

There is a similar concept in Catholic theology called Limbo. Limbo is a place between life and the afterlife. Or, according to various Christian denominations, there is one more concept called Hades, similar to the Islamic concept of Barzakh. Hades is also considered to be an intermediate place between death and the Day of Judgement. Incidentally, In Greek mythology, Hades is both the land of the dead and the god who rules there. My understanding was that Barzakh is closer to Purgatory, but when I learned that Purgatory is a place where, according to Christian belief, people who do not have enough good deeds to qualify for paradise stay here (I believe it is a kind of punishment or process of purification in itself), then I adjusted my understanding to the idea that Purgatory is closer to one more concept in Islam known as *A'raaf* (the Heights). *A'raaf* is a place where people are standing at the edge of both paradise and hell, and they may end up in either of them. This state in itself is a kind of punishment. These people can see both paradise and hell in action, and they are so afraid of hell that just by thinking of ending up there, it causes them pain; ultimately, it is said that they will end up in paradise. *A'raaf* will happen during the Day of Judgement, not between death and the Day of Judgement. As I have mentioned before, these discussions of similarity or difference in religions are out of the scope of this book. I am mentioning these concepts just to show that there is a strong concept of life after death in Abrahamic religions.

Why does everyone wait in Barzakh? It is because Judgement Day cannot happen unless every single human being who lived on this earth is there. The Judgement cannot happen on an individual basis. Why? Firstly, if somebody dies, their deeds (good or bad) may still be ongoing, like a good charity or trust that person formed to help others. Through the trust, that person's good deeds may go on for centuries after their death. Secondly, when a person dies, his friends, family, and enemies are still living. How can he be judged when the people he has dealt with are still living and the consequences of his actions are still playing out? He cannot. Therefore, he will have to wait until all the people he dealt with are there on Judgement Day. And every generation is tied to another generation or several other generations; therefore, all the generations have to be there. Essentially, this means that every single person who lived on this earth will have to be there.

Imagine Person A from the first generation owes a good deed to someone from the first generation itself. Both of these people are dead. However, Person A is expecting a good deed from his or her grandson, who is still alive. When that grandson dies, Person A wants his or her good deed from him; however, that grandson cannot give him or her anything because he is waiting for a good deed from his grandson. This cycle will continue, as someone will still be waiting to get something from the person who is still alive. Therefore, everybody will have to wait until everybody is there on the Day of Judgement. This is a very simple explanation, but in reality, there will be many complications that will make the presence of every individual a necessity for the Day of Judgement to happen.

On Judgement Day, everything will be stopped, and every dead person will be brought back. Everyone who has ever lived will be there, from Adam and Eve to the last child born (although infants will not be judged). You'll start receiving reports of your good deeds and bad deeds. Think of the reports as being like a driving record or credit report: a comprehensive list of every good and bad thing you've ever done. For every action you have taken, there will be consequences; you will be rewarded for good actions and punished for bad ones.

The currency will be different; instead of paper or coins, the currency will consist of deeds. Good deeds count toward rewards, and bad deeds are more like debt—they count against you. A person who did something bad to another person in this world will have to give a good deed to or take a bad deed from that person. But the moment Judgement Day comes, no one will be able to do any more good deeds or atone for past misdeeds.

God will also ask you about your stewardship of the earth. Did you follow the guidance provided or choose to ignore it in favor of convenience? With great power comes great responsibility; did you live up to yours?

Takeaways

---

1. The Day of Judgement is coming.
2. Abrahamic religions believe in the Day of Judgement.
3. Hinduism and Buddhism believe in reincarnation. They also believe in *swarg* (heaven) and *Narg* (hell).
4. It is not about the person who committed injustice; it is about the person to whom the injustice happened.
5. After death people have to wait in a place called Barzakh in Islam and Limbo or Hades in Christianity.
6. On Judgement Day, everyone who lived a life in this world will be brought back to life.

Chapter 4

Why It Is Necessary

Judgement Day is necessary because every action, good or bad, has a consequence, whether that consequence manifests during your lifetime or not.

All the things you've done, no matter how well hidden, will be brought out into the open, and you'll have to give an account for all of them. You will have to answer to every person you've harmed, lied to, stolen from, misled, used, abused, or otherwise wronged—whether they knew about your actions during their lifetime or not. Even your physical body will be present on that day; if you did not treat it well or take care of your health, you will be held accountable. Good deeds you did for other people without their knowledge will also be brought into the light, and those people will be able to express gratitude for your kindness. Nothing will go unnoticed.

All Will Have to Answer for Their Deeds

Similarly, every person who has ever wronged you—openly or in secret—will be held accountable, and they will have to answer to you for their actions. If someone planned against you in their living room or bedroom, you'll find out. You'll know "You had power and planned to do this" or "This is the group or individual who planned against me." There will be no secrets on that day. That is why it's so important to be conscious of how we deal with other people in the present, as the next chapter outlines.

If anyone in a position of power used that power to destroy people, those people will come back and say, "You're the one who did this," or "Why didn't you let me do these things?" If anyone blocked you from achieving something without your knowledge, you'll be able to question the person as to why and how it happened. Many times, people plan things in their drawing rooms or bedrooms, and we never know. But on Judgement Day, every secret plot will be made known.

It's very easy to feel disconnected from high-level concepts and broad descriptions without understanding how they relate to us individually. Here are a few examples that may more clearly paint the picture of how these things apply to our lives.

My coworker's wife was killed by a hit-and-run driver. There was nothing he could do, and he never learned who had taken his wife from this world. On Judgement Day, that driver will be brought before him and will have to answer for his actions.

I used to own a business selling computer parts, and one employee stole a significant amount of inventory over time. It hurt my business very badly. By the time I found out, it was too late to do anything to recover what had been taken. But on Judgement Day, that employee will have to account for his deeds. He did not get away with the theft just because no one caught him.

Hitler did not escape punishment by committing suicide. He will have to answer for all the people who died in camps, in war, and at the hands of the people he commanded. He may have to die for everyone again. I'm not sure exactly how it will happen, but he will have to answer for every single person whose life was taken or harmed by his evil.

There are no exceptions. Every person who ever lived will be judged for their actions, punished for their bad deeds and rewarded for the good. The need to keep the world moving requires that Judgement must not take place here in this world. Of course, there are stories like the story of Prophet Joseph, where a miniature version of the Day of Judgement happened here in this world. Prophet Joseph's ten brothers thought that because they were greater in number, they could do anything to one innocent brother and threw him into a well. Later a woman thought that because she was in a position of power, she could accuse an innocent man without consequence. God ultimately showed that it was He who protected Prophet Joseph in all those trying times, and all the people who tried to harm him had to admit their guilt. I used this story as an analogy of the Day of Judgement. This story could also be used as a triumph of the truth over falsehood or a victory of patience and perseverance over jealousy and cunning. According to Hinduism this story may be Karma in action. Either way there is a sense of Judgement in these kinds of stories. Almost everyone can see these kinds of results when they show the qualities of virtues like prudence, justice, temperance, and courage. These virtues are well defined in Christian literature. However, there is no guarantee that you will see results in this world, and that is why there is a Day of Judgement. That is why this kind of Judgement in this world is the exception rather than the rule.

Again, as I mentioned earlier, it is about the person who was hurt. The Day of Judgement is the only tool God has that can settle all and every injustice that happened in this world.

Takeaways

1. If there is no Day of Judgement, then every-thing becomes meaningless.
2. Every human being deserves to be informed of who caused them pain.
3. Every human has a right to find out whether somebody secretly did good or bad to them.
4. The Day of Judgement is the best tool that will settle all the disputes.

Part Two

Preparation for the Day of Judgement

Just as we have unalienable rights, it is our unalienable responsibility to understand and prepare for the Day of Judgement. As discussed earlier, all major religions agree on two types of sins: major sins and minor sins. However, there is a huge relationship between major and minor sins. Avoiding one may help in avoiding other.

Just as ignorance of the law is not an excuse for breaking it, ignorance of your responsibilities is not an excuse for neglecting them. People often think that preparing for Judgement Day only or primarily requires monitoring our current behavior while keeping an eye toward the future at all times. However, there's more to it than that. Preparing for Judgement Day's demands requires not only changing how we act in the present but also requires addressing our past—what we were taught to accept as good, to value, to turn a blind eye to—and developing our vision for the future while not letting fear of the future paralyze us. The goal of the following chapters is to take a look at all these aspects—our unalienable responsibility to understand and prepare for the Day of Judgement, to explore our past, to understand our present, and to prepare for our future—and to help you understand these aspects so you can prepare for Judgement Day with a clear heart and mind, knowing you've done the best you could in every situation.

Chapter 5

Our Unalienable Responsibilities

The first and foremost unalienable responsibility of human beings is to understand and prepare for the Day of Judgement. Nobody else can prepare for you. You cannot alienate this responsibility to others. The following is a subset of this most important unalienable responsibility. With this being said, let us examine what these unalienable responsibilities are.

The difference between a right and a responsibility is very thin. Often, the rights become responsibilities, and the responsibilities become rights. For example, the right to vote is your right as an adult citizen of the United States of America, and if anybody stops you from exercising this right, you can challenge that in a court. Actually going and voting is your civic responsibility. Nobody can force you to go and vote (at least in the United States of America). What I think the major difference between a right and a responsibility is this: it is incumbent upon you to make sure nobody is in between you and your rights, whereas you have to respond and make an effort to fulfill your responsibility without anybody between you and your responsibility. "Unalienable" simply means that one cannot alienate something from himself or herself. Nobody can take this away from the possessor. There are rights you can surrender or hand over to somebody who can act on your behalf, like giving power of attorney to somebody. However, you cannot give away your unalienable rights to anybody so that they can take care of those rights on your behalf. This is mentioned in the Declaration of Independence: "We hold these truths to be self-evident, that all men are created equal, that they are endowed by their Creator with certain unalienable Rights, that among these are Life, Liberty and the pursuit of Happiness." Similar to these unalienable rights, there are unalienable responsibilities; among those are the following:

1. Responsibility to pray

2. Responsibility to acquire knowledge

3. Responsibility to be healthy

4. Responsibility to spend time wisely

You have a responsibility to your body to eat right; nobody can eat well for you. You have a responsibility to pray; although others can pray for your well-being, no one can pray in your stead. You have a responsibility to acquire knowledge; nobody can learn for you. You have a responsibility to exercise; nobody can lift weights for you. You have a responsibility not to throw trash in your mind, just as you should not throw trash in the environment or put large amounts of junk food into your body. And there is much more. A list of responsibilities alone could be the topic of an entire book, as unalienable responsibilities grow with a person's age, education, and position in society. The more powerful you are, the more responsibilities you have.

Let us explore the above mention unalienable responsibilities in detail.

1. *Responsibility to Pray*

Unalienable responsibilities are at the core of the preparation for the Day of Judgement. The first and the foremost unalienable responsibility is your relationship with your Lord. How much time do you spend contemplating your God? Do you wake up at night and go into deep meditation to get knowledge from your God? Let me tell you one thing in a very straightforward manner: you may spend years and years in trying to understand the concept of anything; you may not be able to understand them. You may think you have mastered whatever field you are in, and then all of a sudden, you will come to a point where you will not be able to solve a minor problem in the same field of which you thought you were a master. The only way you get knowledge is as a gift from God. Am I discouraging you from working hard to become a master in your field? Not at all. What I am saying is to put half the time contemplating your Lord in meditation in prayers, and you will see exponential results. You still have to do your due diligence. As the saying goes, "God helps those who help themselves." "Help themselves" means both that they are praying and they are preparing to achieve their goals. A good achievement is one that makes you humble, not arrogant, and the prayers will make you humble in your achievements. While I am on this subject, let me make it clear that there are people who will spend their life in prayer but will not be able to become humble. This is because they pray mechanically. Their mind is somewhere, but physically they are in prayer. You have to be both mentally and physically present while praying. You may get not only knowledge (even though it is the most important by-product of prayer), but every other material or nonmaterial thing you want you can also get through prayers. Prayers are most important weapons of human beings. You can achieve anything through praying. In fact, the prayers will take care of not almost but every other responsibility. You can consider the other responsibilities as the subsects of the first responsibility. If you are tirelessly working to achieve something, and during this effort you are mindful of your Lord, then this effort becomes a part of your prayers. Then God opens doors of wherever you are trying to go. God will guide you in understanding anything, however difficult that thing might be. God will make things easy for you.

2. Responsibility to Acquire Knowledge

The second unalienable responsibility is taking care of your education. Nobody can learn for you. You have to put in time and effort to learn anything. You have to master memorizing techniques, as memory is the base of knowledge. As mentioned earlier this responsibility is directly connected to the first responsibility, prayer. God will help you understand which field is good for you. He will also make you understand the concepts of that field.

3. Responsibility to Be Healthy

I wanted to say that taking care of your health is an unalienable responsibility; however, I realized that somebody else can also take care of your health, like nurses and caregivers. Therefore, taking care of your health will not be an unalienable responsibility if somebody else can take care of you. Due to this reason, I am using the words "be healthy." Be healthy by exercising. Nobody can exercise for you. Be healthy by eating healthy food. Nobody can chew healthy food for you. Be healthy by following a good, consistent routine. Being healthy is one of the most important ways we can prepare for Judgement Day. On Judgement Day, you'll have to answer to every entity you've harmed, including your physical body. If you did not treat it well, you will have to answer to your body, just as you will to everyone else your actions affected.

Being healthy is also important because it affects how you deal with other people. If you have poor posture, it may cause pain that makes you snap at others or lose your temper when you would have been calm otherwise. If you're feeling angry about something that someone said or did, it can be helpful to exercise, take a walk, or do something else so you don't immediately react. Take some time to ask yourself why something bothered you. Was it really that person's actions or words, or is there an underlying cause, like pain, low energy from eating junk food, or exhaustion from skipping breakfast?

4. *Responsibility to Spend Time Mindfully*

I am pretty sure spending time mindfully is an unalienable responsibility. Nobody else can spend time mindfully for you. Here, "mindfully" has two possible meanings. Firstly, you should be mindful of your whereabouts—where are you standing, sitting, or lying in a particular moment of time. Secondly, you should be mindful of what is going on in a particular moment of time. You should have all of your attention on what is going on.

Takeaways

1. Preparing for the Day of Judgement is our unalienable responsibility.
2. This unalienable responsibility is comprised of more unalienable responsibilities.
3. Among those unalienable responsibilities are the following:
    a. Responsibility to pray
    b. Responsibility to gain knowledge
    c. Responsibility to be healthy
    d. Responsibility to spend time mindfully

Chapter 6

Addressing the Past

A Bank Account of Deeds

As I mentioned earlier, a record of your life is like a driving record or a credit report, a comprehensive list of every good and bad thing you've ever done from the moment you were born to the moment you're reading these words. For every action you have taken, there will be consequences. You will be rewarded for good actions, and you will be punished for bad ones.

Think of your actions as being bank-account withdrawals or deposits. When you do good things, the balance in your account increases. When you do bad things, the balance in your account decreases, and you'll have to do something good to make up for it. Your goal is to keep a positive balance in your account so you can always withdraw, the same way you would keep some savings in reserve for emergencies.

It's simply a fact of life that you will do bad deeds at some point, no matter how good a person you are. Sometimes you might face a situation where you have to lie, or you may unintentionally harm another person through a thoughtless act. If you do a bad thing, you should do some good deeds to balance it out, such as giving to charities, helping other people avoid getting into the same situation you did, or helping someone get out of a bad situation. Again, think of your bank account—you want to keep a positive balance so there's always a safety cushion if you do something wrong. If you have made many withdrawals in the past, simply take steps to make more deposits than withdrawals starting now.

You should also keep track of good deeds others have done for you. If someone shows you kindness, look for an opportunity to show kindness to someone else. If something is given to you, make note of the amount and try to reciprocate—pass it on to charity or someone else in need. That's not to say that you should never accept gifts or acts of kindness; rather, the point is that you should also try to pass on these kinds of deeds to others.

We must always be conscious about what we are doing because those actions will come out in the open on Judgement Day. Every moment is being recorded.

However, the point of this is not to strike fear in you. You should not become so worried and so obsessed over every tiny detail of your behavior that you become paralyzed or give up on keeping a positive balance. I'm going to suggest something counter to popular opinion: don't be afraid to make mistakes.

Don't Be Afraid to Make Mistakes

I'll say that again: don't be afraid to make mistakes. Much of life—our parents, our schooling, and the media—trains us not to make mistakes, but we often lose the game of life by only playing on the defensive. If you simply live by a set of good rules, you can move freely without having to worry about missteps along your journey.

What is a set of good rules? Here are some examples:

- The Golden Rule: Treat everyone as you want to be treated.
- Treat your body right; eat healthy foods and exercise.
- Pray and gain knowledge as much as possible.
- Set financial rules for your circumstances, such as saving a certain percentage of your income or adhering to a certain budget each month.
- Stick to your daily routine; wake up on time, and go to sleep on time.
- Take care of relationships; give your time to everyone. Don't have false pretenses, putting one friend down while raising another up or spending time with someone only because you want something from them.
- Be good to your neighbors.
- Give your children enough of your time, and teach them how to live.
- Follow the law.
- Respect others.

And so on.

Life will bring challenges. That is inevitable. You don't need to think of all these rules constantly, worrying, "Oh, I have to be good to my neighbors today and spend time with my kids and spend time with friends." Just do your best. No one can do more than that, right?

You *will* make mistakes. It's a part of life. The key is to follow a good set of rules consistently and take things one day at a time. Do your best in the moment. When you make a mistake, repent and seek forgiveness from the person you harmed or affected. If you're not sure how to make up for something, just ask! Go to that person and say, "How can I correct this?" or "How can I make things right?" Don't beat yourself up about it or let guilt torture you. Just remind yourself, "I made a mistake, and I have made things right. I am not going to make this same mistake again."

To be clear, living freely doesn't mean you should throw caution to the wind. You shouldn't live so carelessly that you don't try to rectify mistakes, but you shouldn't fear mistakes so much that your fear keeps you from living your life.

Again, a set of good rules is not the same as some checklist to be rigidly adhered to. Life is like a game:

you must constantly adapt and improvise. You have to keep your eye on the ball—but in life, you never know where the ball is! In fact, sometimes you don't even know *what* it is. When you're driving, the car may be your ball; you have to focus on staying in your lane, making sure you don't collide with any other vehicles, and going in the right direction. When you get home, the ball may change to something else, like cleaning, helping the kids with their homework, spending time with your spouse, or preparing a meal. Just make sure you're giving all you can to that particular moment in time. Also, by keeping an eye on these different and important balls, you are actually keeping an eye on the big ball that is the Day of Judgement. When you have good rules in place, you can move freely and confidently. If you make a mistake, seek forgiveness. It's as simple as that.

Evaluate Your Results and What You've Been Taught Early in Life

It is important to evaluate your results and take an honest look at your way of thinking. In our first eighteen years or so of life, we usually don't live *our* lives; we live our parents' lives, our cultures' lives, the lives of the people who have authority over us. After that, when you're able to see clearly, you have to go back and challenge what was impressed upon you. Reflect on your childhood and adolescence. What was good? What was not so good?

Things you were taught to believe were objectively good or bad may not have been. Maybe your parents taught you to respect rich people or taught you not to challenge or question authority or taught you to always expect bad things to happen. Maybe your culture taught you to be small-minded without your realizing it. Or your culture may have taught you that certain things were bad when those things weren't bad. It's important to reexamine the things you've taken for granted, taking an honest look at what you've been taught.

Your heart may have been damaged by your culture's influence or your parents' influence. A lot may not have been good. You shouldn't take everything for granted as right. If something *was* good, you should appreciate it as such. But understand that not everything may have been.

For example, many times, culture teaches us to save every penny and be careful of every small thing. But whenever major opportunities arise, we ignore them or are not prepared to take advantage of them.

It's like teaching us to pick up every penny but not hundred-dollar bills.

Think of a basketball game. The importance of practice is touted over and over again. Much importance is placed on wearing the right shoes and the right socks, having the right form during practice, running laps, and so on. These are important to a degree, but the most important thing is winning the game! When the game is being played, shoes and socks don't do anything to affect the outcome; the ball and the person working with the ball are what matter. If someone performs terribly in practice but wins the game, he is celebrated. If someone plays flawlessly in every practice but bombs during the match, he is put down. Don't get me wrong; practice is important, but practice should be focused toward winning the actual match. Practice should not be just for the sake of showing that you are practicing.

Similarly, culture may teach us to lose sight of things that we ourselves truly value. If we are trained to focus so much on material things that we discount the value of other aspects of life, then when it comes time to pick between money, careers, and love, we end up picking money or career—when neither may not be the most important thing to us.

In essence, culture can often teach us to miss the forest for the trees. It's important to evaluate what we've been taught so we can recognize what is good and what is not.

In Eastern cultures, the status quo remains the same because people don't question anything. But you must feel free to question authority and teachings. Question how your culture dealt with someone in the past or treats people in the present. Question why bad things are considered bad and why good things are considered good. Even question whether laws are right. During World War II, it was illegal in Germany to offer aid or comfort to a Jew. Because it was a law, did that make it right?

You may have to practice patience while waiting for answers to come, and there may be consequences for going against popular opinion. Prophet Abraham was thrown into fire for questioning the authorities of his time, but the fire was made peaceful, and he was not harmed. Of course, your consequences may not be made into peace in the same way, but it is important to question things so that your life—and society as a whole—can progress in the right direction.

Practice Critical Thinking

As the previous section illustrates, it's important to practice critical thinking. What exactly *is* critical thinking? It means that you're always adjusting to new information. When you get new information, your opinion should change.

Sometimes you may think something is correct based on the information you have at that point— knowledge you gained from family, friends, media, books, or other sources. Then when more information comes, you should adjust your position accordingly. Your thinking shouldn't be set in stone. As Muhammad Ali said, "The man who views the world at fifty the same as he did at twenty has wasted thirty years of his life."

Think of the story of Prophet Abraham. Prophet Abraham at first thought the moon was God because that was the information he had. Then the moon disappeared, and he realized it was not God. Then the sun came, and Abraham thought, "The sun is God." It was bigger and shone brighter than the moon. But the sun disappeared, and he realized it was not God. Ultimately, God spoke to him and said, "I am your God," and Abraham realized it was true. God helps those people who make wrong choices with good intentions. Even though Abraham made wrong choices with the moon and sun, his intentions were good; because he adapted his position based on the new information given to him, he finally found the true God. Once you start questioning and using critical thinking, the answers will come.

Takeaways

1. Every good deed by humans is recorded as a positive balance in their account.
2. Every bad deed by humans is recorded as a negative balance in their account.
3. Keep on doing good deeds so that your positive balance is much more than negative balance.
4. Have a good set of rules in place.
5. Practice critical thinking.
6. Evaluate your past so that your future is on a good foundation.

Chapter 7

*Handling the Present
and Your Day to Day*

Protect Your Soul; Don't Burden It

It is important to protect your soul by not doing things that will burden your soul. Think of it this way: your soul is like water. Pure water will take on the color of anything that you put into it. If you put dye in a glass of water, the water will become darker and darker, cloudier and cloudier, until it is the color of the dye. But if you put pure water in it, it will become purer and purer until it's pure and clear again. Putting bad thoughts or feelings into your mind affects your soul the same way that the dye affects water. Be careful what you're exposing yourself to—the people you spend time with, the places you go, the media you consume—and limit your contact with things that burden your soul.

God Will Test You—Pass the Test

As mentioned before, life brings challenges. Sometimes God Himself will test you, but being tested is a good thing. If you pass the test, your rank will be raised, and you'll have a greater reward. If you fail the test, your rank will be lowered. Just do your best to understand the situation, and handle it as well as you can.

The test can come up randomly. Most of us do not even know that we are going through a test, let alone passing it. This is where we must practice finding out what is going on and act accordingly.

You can prepare for tests by gaining knowledge—reading books of wisdom and learning from the lives of good people. Patience is also key; even if a test seems to last unbearably long, know that you will get through it. No test lasts forever.

Like the tests in school, your tests will be on the same level you are. If you're in first grade, the test will be given at a first-grade level. You'll never be given a third-grade test when you're in first grade. If you pass, you'll go on to second grade. If you don't pass, you may have to repeat first grade. The important thing is to learn from failure and do a better job the next time.

You can think of the tests as being like the chutes in Chutes and Ladders. You might be walking along one day, thinking you're doing a great job, then fall down a chute to a lower level. It will require time and patience to work your way back up to where you were, but when you encounter that chute again, you'll know to avoid it, and you'll be able to pass it the second time around.

Don't Get Upset or Angry Easily

In a way, it is helpful for you to be like a good politician. Politicians don't get upset or angry very easily. People insult them, accuse them, blame them, and charge them, and politicians still respond calmly and collectedly. In the same way, you have to make a conscious choice not to let things people say or do upset you. As Eleanor Roosevelt said, "No one can make you feel inferior without your consent." No one on this earth can make you upset unless you let them.

Practice Patience

It is critical to practice patience. It is not always best to speak your mind or take action right away. Many times, problems resolve themselves if we wait. We must develop the habit of letting time pass before reacting to a situation. The saying "Sleep on it" exists for a reason.

Imagine sauce falling on a white cloth. Sometimes it is better to wait a moment before immediately starting to clean it off. Starting the wrong way with the wrong cleaning method can make the stain spread more or become more deeply embedded in the fabric. The same concept applies to our own lives. It may be better to let some time pass before responding to a situation.

Oftentimes, children think something is of paramount importance—a matter of life and death—but their parents know it's not a big deal (and children realize that as they grow up). Think of the young children who scream when their peas and carrots touch at dinnertime. Adults face this too. Politicians often paint issues as more urgent than they really are to influence people for personal gain. A sense of urgency may be needed in some situations, but it should be an appropriate level of urgency. Sometimes taking a step back and letting some time pass before you react can help you understand things more clearly and choose the best course of action.

Building this important habit won't happen overnight. It will take prayer, study, and conscious effort. But in time, you will start to develop the quality of taking your time and thinking before reacting.

It is also important to practice patience because many times, we are wrong without realizing it! Resist the urge to blame others. After reflecting on the situation, you may realize, "I was the one who was creating the problem."

Say you're angry with your boss for criticizing you. It is easy to rage against your boss, feeling unappreciated, unjustly reprimanded, or treated with rudeness. But the cause may be that you were the one not coming in on time, not taking your job seriously, or unwittingly causing a problem in other areas of the company. Your anger can blind you to your contribution to an issue. That's why it's important to see everything as clearly as possible. Practicing patience, taking a moment to step back before responding, will help clear your vision.

You may simply find that you need to exert more effort waking up on time, showering quickly, and getting to your job. If the root cause is trouble sleeping, you may find you need to do exercises to sleep more soundly and wake up on time. Again, taking care of your physical health is incredibly important, as neglected health can become a source of problems with other people. These are all things within your control. Practicing patience will give you clearer vision so you can address the root cause of a situation and resolve it in the best way possible.

Tolerating Cruelty or Injustice Is Not Patience

It must be noted that tolerating cruelty or injustice is not the same as patience. You should tackle injustice head-on and face the consequences. Suppose your boss was outright harassing you at work, bullying you, humiliating you, or setting you up for failure. You should confront that. A potential consequence may be that you lose your job, or you may have to fight through layers of bureaucracy before anything changes. But tolerating your boss's injustice is not the right kind of patience. Showing patience in facing the consequences could be the right kind of patience.

In situations where it's unclear where the fault lies—you might be right; you might be wrong—it is better not to take action immediately. Take some time to think over things before responding. But in a situation where there's a clear injustice—someone taking advantage of their position or power, for example—then you should take action and handle the consequences as they come.

Don't Judge Others

Finally, don't judge others. You might say, "I would never do that," but then God will test you, and you'll do the same thing. You never know a person's situation or circumstances. We have to have patience with others and mind our own affairs rather than judging the actions of others.

Takeaways

1. Don't burden your soul.
2. God will test you.
3. Pass the test with prayer and with patience, as no test will be beyond your ability and will not go on forever.
4. Tolerating injustice or cruelty is not patience.
5. Do not judge others.

Chapter 8

Preparing for the Future

Build Your Vision

Hindsight is twenty-twenty. Things that may have been uncertain or hazy at the time seem obvious when we look back on them. But knowing a solution after the problem has occurred isn't helpful. We must make our foresight twenty-twenty as well.

How? You have to strengthen your vision. Vision comes from acquiring knowledge: reading the books of wisdom, going to prayer and worship, learning from good people's lives, and strengthening your relationship with God. Knowledge gives the mind different scenarios to reference so we can identify what situations we are in, distinguish between right and wrong, and discern how to react correctly. In short, knowledge lets you see things in front of you as clearly as possible with twenty-twenty foresight.

In order to start seeing clearly, we have to spend time with Almighty God. Preparing for some other thing is entirely different than preparing for the Day of Judgement. For other preparations you know the exact demands or the types of subjects that are covered for some exam, and you can assign a time to understand the demands or practice questions and answers covering those subjects. But preparation for the Day of Judgement can be very comprehensive because testing can take place anytime, anywhere. Finding out that a test is going on itself needs understanding. Many times, we would not be able to even find out that we just failed the test, when unknowingly we just insulted one poor person or one weak person. To understand what exactly is going on, we need vision. Assigning a time to prepare for the Day of Judgement is very important, but again, because there is no fixed syllabus, we have to pray to Almighty God to let us have the foresight to understand where we are standing and where we are going. We have to understand that nobody is able to influence us to perform acts that are beneficial to them. This is very important because these are the very situations when we become a kind of slave to those people under whose influence we are living our lives. We cannot decide ourselves what is right or what is wrong. We just think that whatever they say right is right, and whatever they say wrong is wrong. These people will not come for our help on the Day of Judgement. While on this topic, I want to make it clear that good mentors are like beacons; having a good mentor is like having a guide who can provide you with great advice. You should surround yourself with such mentors. Again, to find the difference between selfless and selfish mentors, you need prayers. Only God can help you out. Depending on your sincerity, God will bring you to great mentors.

Have an Infrastructure

Like a good infrastructure of a good city, we should have an infrastructure of sound principles in our lives. Imagine when a storm or heavy rain occurs in a well-designed city. The citizens hardly feel the impact of the storm or heavy rain. The city has already taken care of designing all the roads, sewer lines, storm drains, et cetera, on good, sound design principles. The infrastructure has to be timeless. Similarly, if we have an infrastructure of a sound relationship with Almighty God; a sound education of good principles; a great, healthy lifestyle with which we take care of our bodies; and care for the environment we dwell in, we can handle the storms of life. As discussed earlier, surround yourselves with a group of people who understand your values and who can increase your vision with their vision.

Don't Worry about the Future

Although it is important to prepare for Judgement Day and be conscious about how you live your life, you shouldn't worry unnecessarily about the future. It's easy to feel overwhelmed in these tumultuous times when there seem to be more terrible things happening in the world than ever before. But the key is not to let these events weigh on your mind to an unhealthy degree.

Think of it like being an actor in a movie. Big things may be going on to bring this moving into reality. The producer will work toward what he is supposed to work for, the director is making sure the direction is as perfect as possible, but the movie is centered on the lead actor. The actor needs to focus only on delivering his lines well, and he'll get to the end of the movie. The lead actor don't have to know about what is going on the side of production or the side of direction. In the same way, we shouldn't worry so much about the things in the world beyond our control. We must keep our focus on our lives and our conduct, taking each day as it comes. Of course the lead actor can learn about how the production and direction works, and that knowledge can be beneficial for the actor to work hand in hand with producer and director, but ultimately he is responsible for his performance.

Give your best preparation and relax. Imagine that you're on a train going from New York to Chicago. If you start worrying about how the train will make it through all the places in between, you can work yourself into a nervous wreck. You can say to yourself, "How will this train get all the way to Chicago?" You can fret over the obstacles the train encounters on its journey: "A bridge is coming up— what if the bridge breaks? What if we fall in the river when we cross over it?" You can stress over delays or schedule changes: "The train is stopped at a station right now. Will it start going again?" You have to understand that the train is on its intended track. There is a whole infrastructure making this train journey possible. There are so many people working hard to make this journey go smoothly and to make sure you reach your destination safely. It will get to Chicago, whether or not you worry. You'll enjoy the trip much more if you simply enjoy the view, taking in the landscapes and scenes as they pass by.

Your life progresses in the same way. Don't worry too much about how you'll get from point A to point B. Of course, you should plan and prepare all you can, just as you'd buy a ticket and pack your belongings before getting on a train. But once you've done what's within your power, you shouldn't worry anymore. Take heart knowing that you've done everything you can; then sit back and enjoy the ride.

Use your time wisely rather than worrying too much and wasting time only in thinking how bad the situation can go. Start preparing for whatever task is in your hand. Due diligence is the key to success. Remember the story of Hagar, Ibram's wife. Ibram left his wife and child in the desert to wait for his return. When the child needed water after they had run out, Hagar didn't sit around doing nothing, saying, "God will take care of us." She ran around between the hills, looking all over for water, but she found none.

Finally, a small spring came up where the child was, and they had all the water they needed. We must adopt the same approach; we should look all around for opportunities, do what we can, and then leave the rest to God. There is a difference between worrying to death and struggling to find solutions.

Here's another example. Imagine being the president of a country. Presidents don't worry about the entire term of their leadership all at once; they just take things day by day. They will definitely have an agenda for the whole term. Yet they follow the schedule set up for them on a daily basis, go to meetings, and participate fully in the moment. We have to do the same thing. God has set up a schedule for us, so we just go where we're called and participate as best we can in that moment in time. We keep an eye toward the future but don't let it burden us.

In short, don't worry about the future. Just wake up each day, and do your best to handle things as they come up. Use all the tools and knowledge you have available, and know that the rest is in God's hands.

Takeaways

1. Build your foresight to see clearly at twenty-twenty.
2. Have an infrastructure.
3. Don't worry too much about future; just do your due diligence.
4. Have good mentors.

Final Thoughts

Judgement Day is coming. While it may seem far away, it will come in an instant. It will be as real as this book in your hands, as real as the pages in your hands, as real as everything you see, hear, and feel around you.

Just as we have unalienable rights, we have an unalienable responsibility to prepare for that day. We have a responsibility to treat others well—to treat them with kindness and respect, as we want to be treated. We also have a responsibility to take care of our physical bodies, to eat foods that increase our health rather than detracting from it, and to exercise regularly. Far more than we realize, our physical health can affect how well we react to situations in the moment.

We have a responsibility to do more good deeds than bad, the same way a bank account must have more deposits than withdrawals. We have a responsibility to exercise critical thinking, protect our souls from unnecessary burdens, practice patience, and refrain from judging others since we do not know their circumstances. We have a responsibility to develop twenty-twenty foresight through prayer, studying the books of wisdom and learning from the lives of good people.

Lastly, although we are preparing for the future, we have a responsibility not to worry ourselves to death *about* the future. Once we have done all we can—put a good set of principles in place and done everything within our power—we must place the rest in God's hands.

We are not on this earth merely to do as we please, to cheat, lie, and escape in death. We will be punished for our bad deeds and rewarded for our good deeds after death. In the same way, everyone who has ever cheated, defeated, lied to, misled, used, abused, or otherwise wronged us will have to answer for their actions on Judgement Day.

I hope this book will encourage you to take a look at the way you are living your life in the present, as if you were looking in a mirror. Knowing what is coming, do you feel content with the way you are living, or are there aspects of your life that you would like to change? Do you feel ready for Judgement Day, or are there steps you need to take to prepare? Only you know the answer.

References

All the stories or quotes I used in this book are part of common knowledge.

Every story, definition of religious terms, or quote I used in this book is either something I read at various points throughout my adult life, heard in sermons or lectures, or discussed with my elders in family gatherings. I consider these all to be common knowledge. Most of the stories are so common that there are movies made on the topics. There may be a few religious definitions that may not be very common, but they still can be found in dozens, if not hundreds, of places. Therefore, even those definitions fall under the domain of common knowledge.

I intend to keep on improving the content of this book. During those improvements, if needs arise, I may have to provide citations.

www.ingramcontent.com/pod-product-compliance
Lightning Source LLC
Chambersburg PA
CBHW070525030426
42337CB00016B/2112